The Povey Bros.
Stained Glass Windows
of Central Christian Church
in Walla Walla, Washington

The Povey Bros.
Stained Glass Windows
of Central Christian Church
in Walla Walla, Washington

Barbara Beito

The Povey Bros. Stained Glass Windows
of Central Christian Church
in Walla Walla, Washington.

Published in the United States of America
2014.

Library of Congress Cataloging-in-Publication Data
available

ISBN: 978-0-9886155-1-9

Available from Amazon.com, CreateSpace.com
and other retail outlets.

In celebration of
my mother Winifred's 91st year

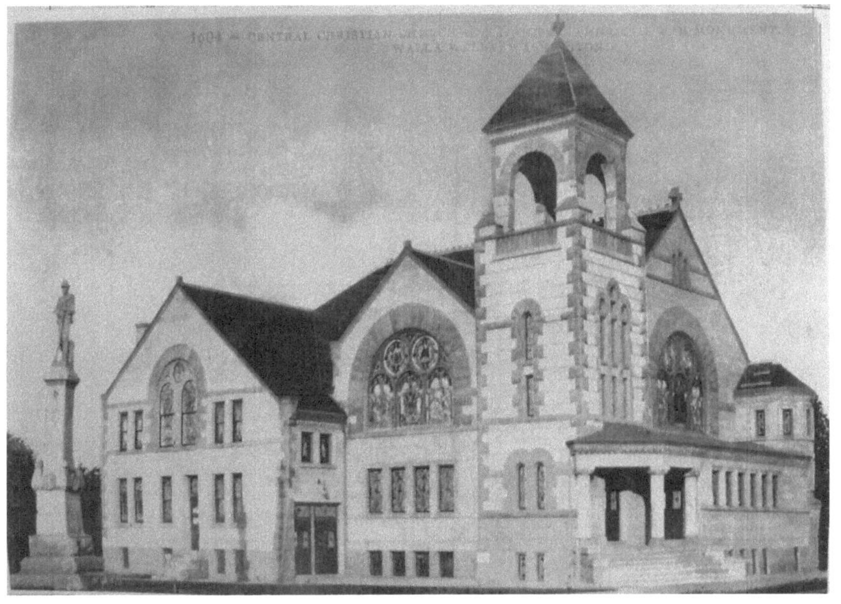

Photo about 1910, courtesy of Central Christian Church

Special thanks to Patton McKinney, Custodian,
and Floralyn Taylor, Office Manager

The Early 1900s

The cornerstone at Central Christian Church, donated by Wylie Monument Company, was laid November 11, 1905 on the site of what had previously been a livery stable. The first service in the building was September 9, 1906 and the church was dedicated on March 10, 1907.

Church records (A) document payments were made to Povey Bros. Glass Company of Portland, Oregon for all the windows in the church on February 7, May 28, and December 30, 1907. The Central Christian Church ledger for Fiscal Year 1906 records the design and production of the Povey windows cost $1,307.51: freight from Portland was $10.69. Stone for the outside was purchased from Tenino Stone Quarries, Inc. The entire expense for the building including the lighting system, large pipe organ, classrooms, windows and minister's study was approximately $50,000. The "preacher and powerhouse" behind the building of Central Christian Church at Palouse and Alder Streets in Walla Walla was Morton Gregory. Mr. Gregory served from August 1904 until he resigned in September 1907: his annual salary was $1,600.(B).

An advertisement in the 1889 Portland City Directory reads "Povey Bros. Art Stained Glass for Churches and Dwellings, 42 Second St., Portland, Oregon". Founded the previous year by brothers David and John Povey, by the turn of the century Povey Bros. was known as the "Tiffany of the Northwest". David was responsible for design and artwork, and John did the glazing and leading. A third brother, George, later joined them and became the company's accountant and business manager.

Their glass was imported from England, and also obtained from Kokomo Indiana: their windows often incorporating hand-painted glass pieces, "jewels" of small thickly cut faceted pieces of glass in rich colors, and different types and textures of glass including crackle, rippled, granite-textured, opalescent and machine-rolled. Grape clusters, roses, lilies, birds and dogwood were frequent motifs. Another notable feature was use of clear glass in the background to allow light pass through the windows on overcast days. These characteristics of Povey glasswork can be observed in windows throughout Central Christian Church.

Povey windows were not signed until the early 1920s, when the brothers responded to imitators passing off their work as the Povey's. David Povey died in 1923 and the business was sold in 1930 (C). It was good to be allowed access to church records and to locate original documentation of the purchase of windows to establish the windows were indeed the work of the Povey Bros.

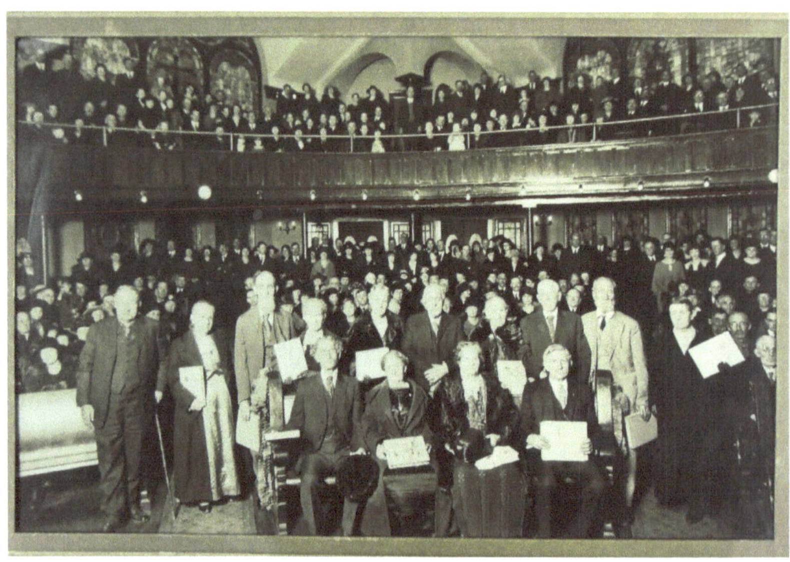

The Sanctuary, around 1910. Photo by The Arnold Studio, courtesy of Central Christian Church.

The 3 stained glass windows to the left of the entry doors in the preceding picture were relocated when the church was remodeled in 1960. They were inset into the second floor of a wall separating the sanctuary from the overflow/annex area.

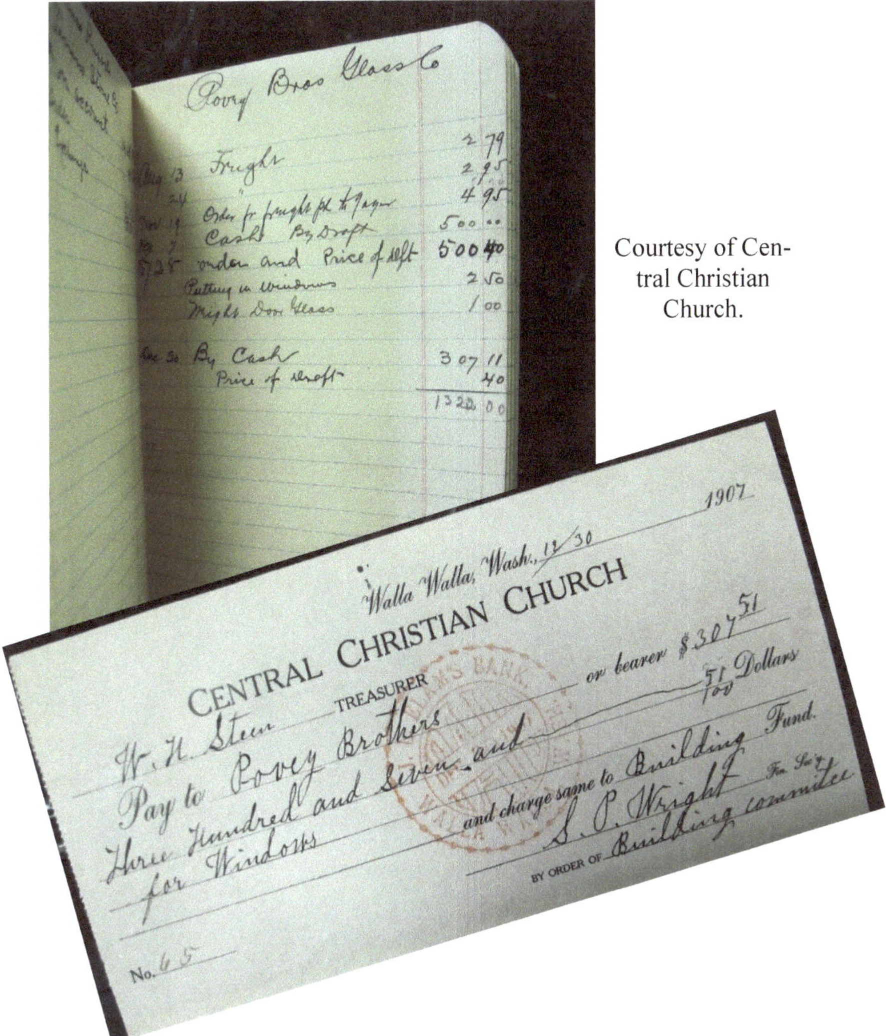

Povey Bros Glass Co

Aug 13	Freight	2 79
24	"	2 95
	Order for freight pd to Pagne	4 95
	Cash By Draft	500 ..
	order and Price of draft	500 40
	Putting in windows	2 50
	Might Door Glass	1 00
Dec 30	By Cash	307 11
	Price of draft	40
		1322 00

1907

Walla Walla, Wash., 12/30

CENTRAL CHRISTIAN CHURCH

W. H. Steen TREASURER

Pay to Povey Brothers or bearer $307.51

Three Hundred and Seven and 51/100 Dollars

for Windows

and charge same to Building Fund.

S. P. Wright Fin. Sec'y

BY ORDER OF Building committee

No. 65

Courtesy of Central Christian Church.

WINDOW ORIENTATION

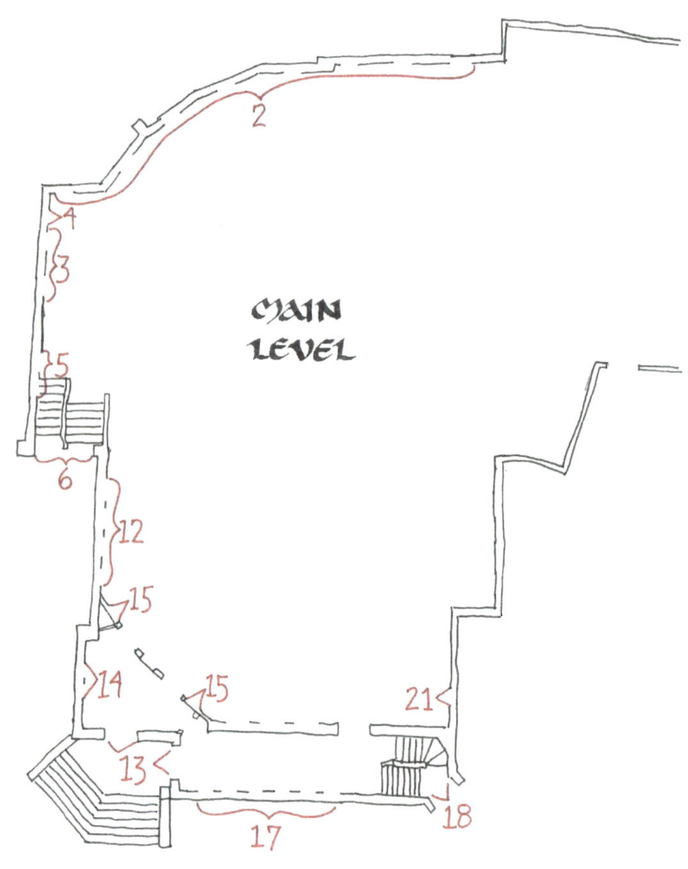

PALOUSE ST.

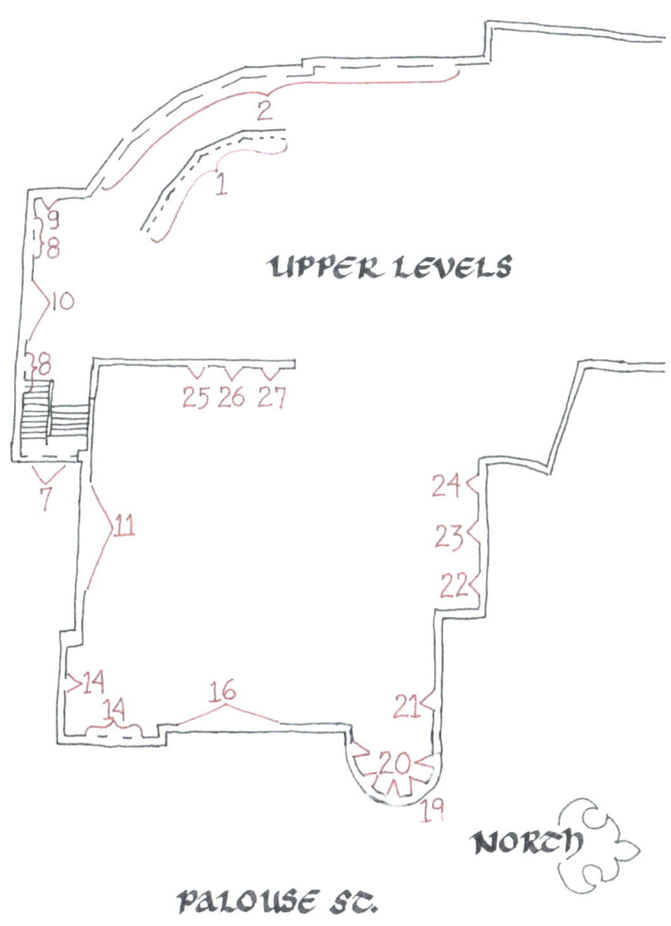
2
1
9
8
10
UPPER LEVELS
8
25 26 27
7
11
24
23
22
14
14
16
21
20
19
NORTH
PALOUSE ST.

A Century Later

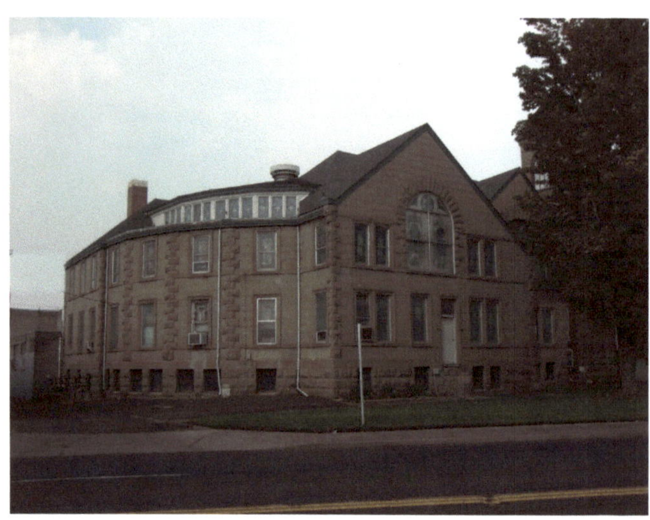

From Alder Street

The four story building includes a basement that has external windows which are leaded but not stained, and an attic that features an arch of twelve 32 pane windows incorporating a central fleur-de-leis (1) that follow the curve of the building.

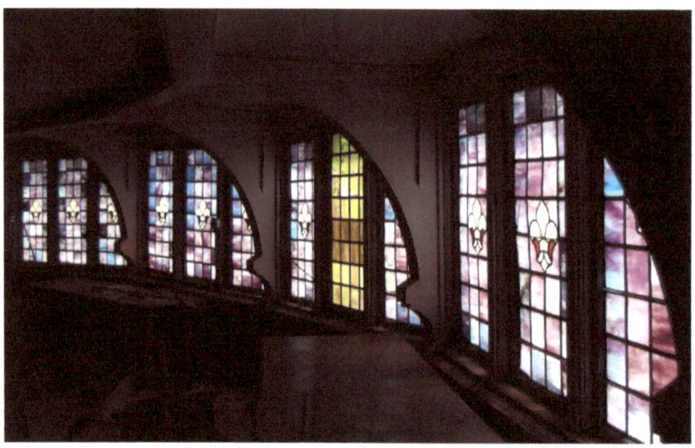

1. Attic, or third floor.

The first and second floors share the two-story sanctuary, and were remodeled in 1960 when the half-circle balcony was reduced in size, classrooms were added, and doors separating the main nave from the secondary were replaced.

The external windows for classrooms on the second floor as well as the little chapel, minister's study and offices on the first, which run along the alley-side and make the curve into Alder Street, are the same design on both floors. (2) There are several windows with slight color variations.

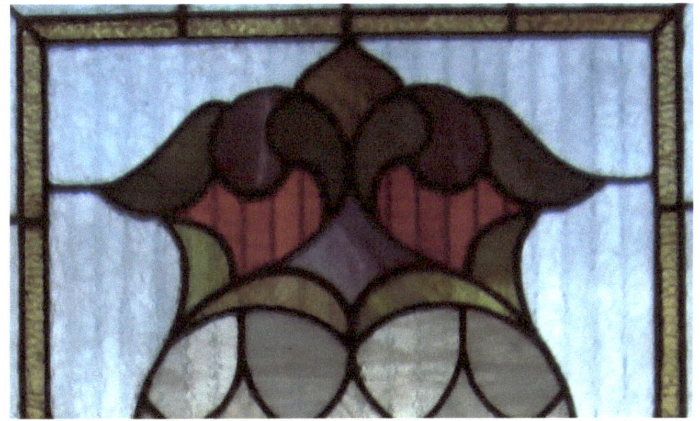

2.Detail, top

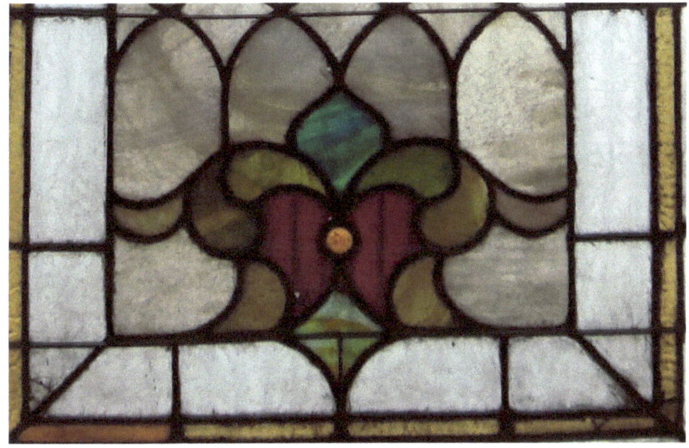

2. Detail, bottom

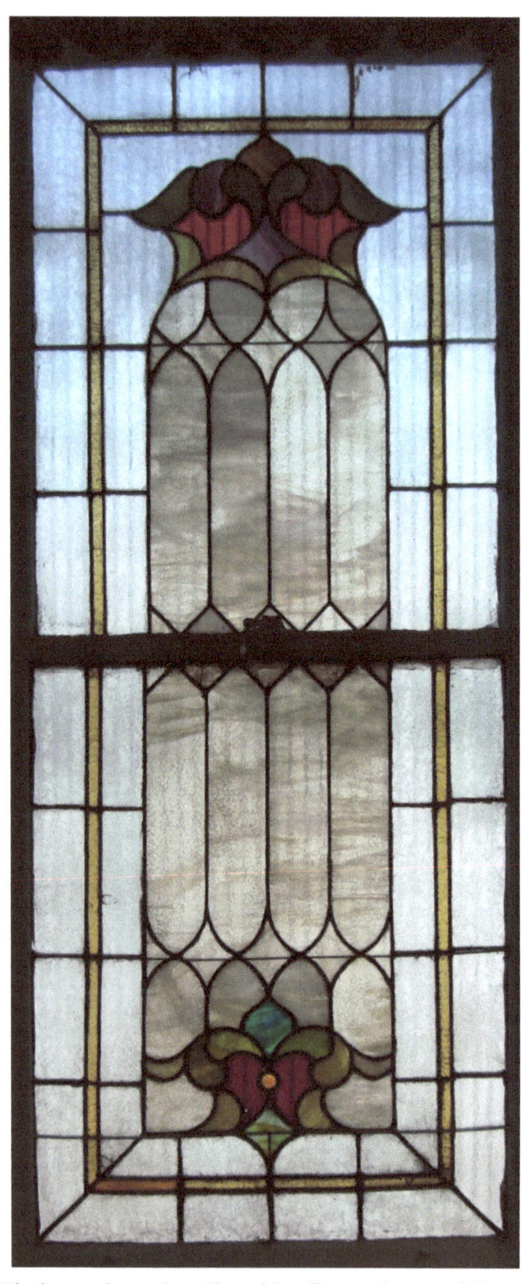

2. Windows along the alley side, first and second floors

A 'jog' on the Alder side of the church encloses office space, hallway and stairwell with double doors to the outside and transom windows facing East on the first floor, and on the second, stairs and a prayer room that face South.

The first floor windows on the Southwest corner of the jog are more elaborate than the others: two are original (3) but one is a combination of two different styles (4): the window on the west side of the jog matches those on the west side of the building (2).

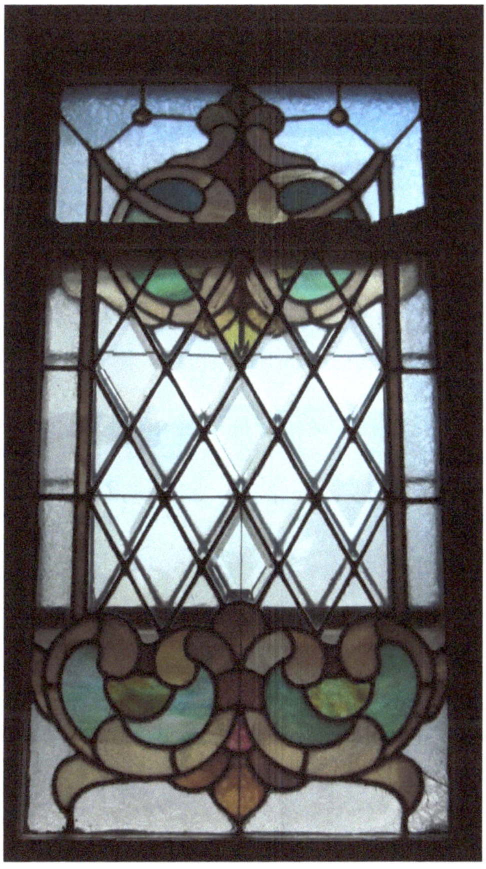

3. Window open

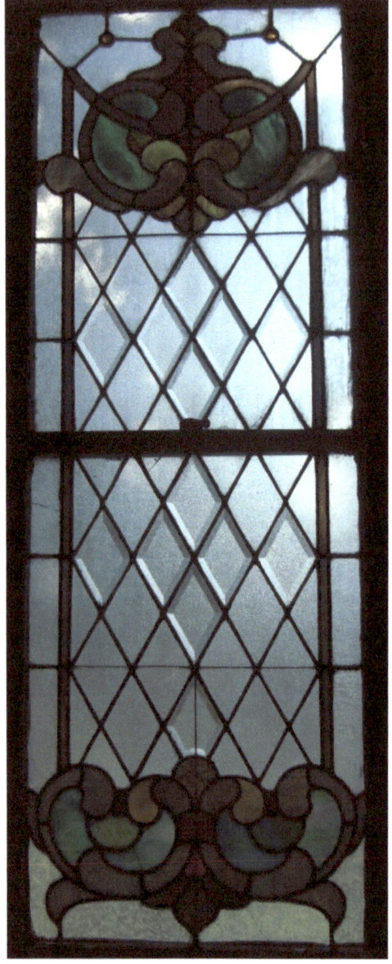

< 3.Window closed

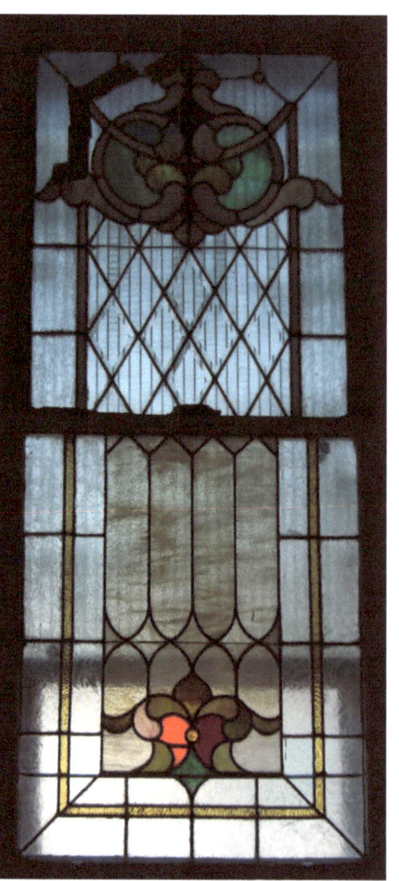

4. Combined window>

A grill covers a transom window over a door in the middle of the south side of the jog. The two windows to the East of the door provide light for the steps to the second floor balcony (5).

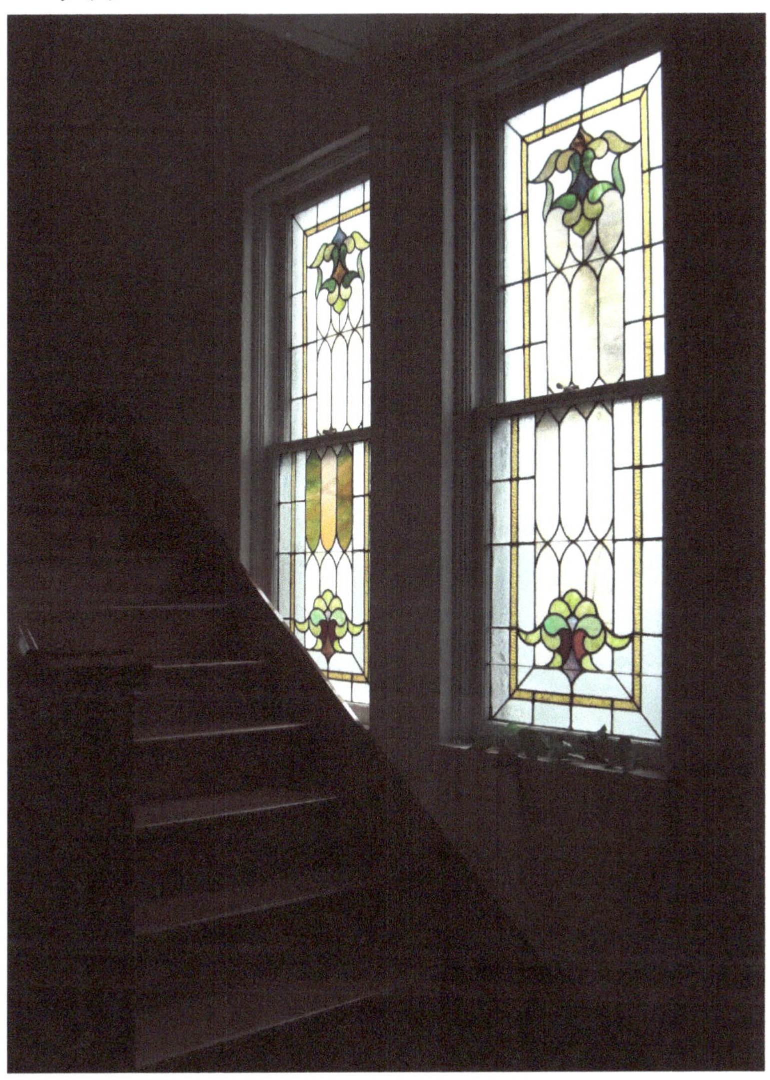

5. First floor stairwell

A first floor exit door opens from the ground level, and a second door is an exit door from the basement under the stairs to the balcony. Matching transom windows (6) top both double door exits as seen below. Two shorter windows above the exit doors on the second floor west side of the jog light the stair landing and counterbalance the doors (7).

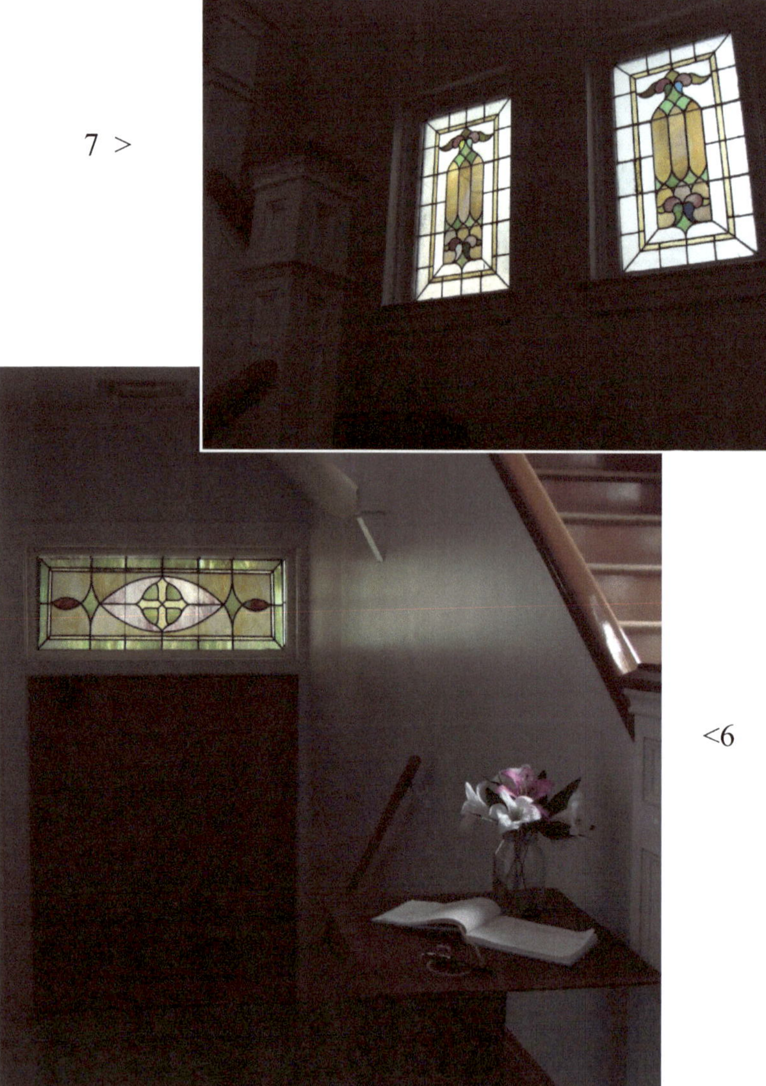

On the second floor, all four of the smaller windows around the large central panel of windows are similar to windows on the alley-side and those around the stairwell but they have three center panes instead of four, and different motif panes (8): one window on the east side of the jog is a combination (9).

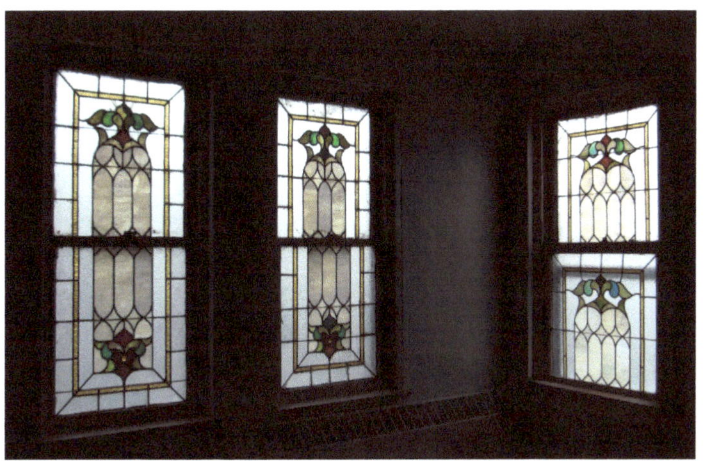

For a quick comparison of similar windows:

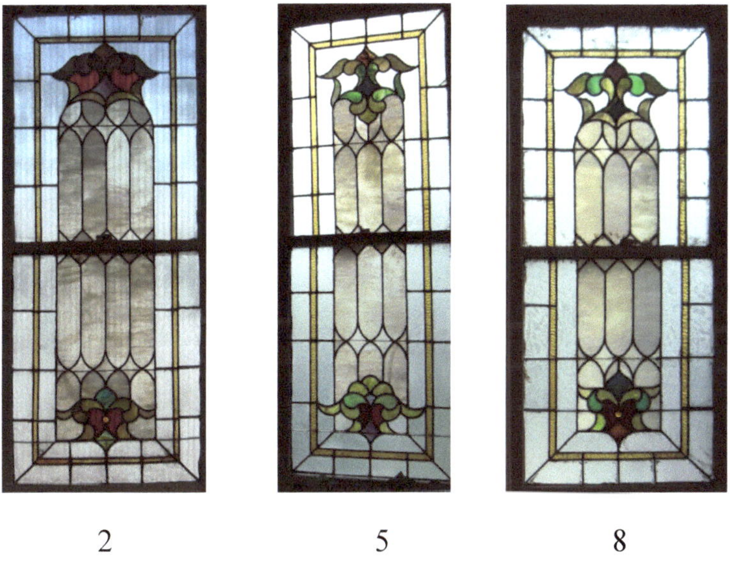

2 5 8

The biggest window in the 'jog' is comprised of two arched windows surmounted by a round window that features a dogwood blossom (10). The use of different color and texture combinations as well as leading techniques is quite effective.

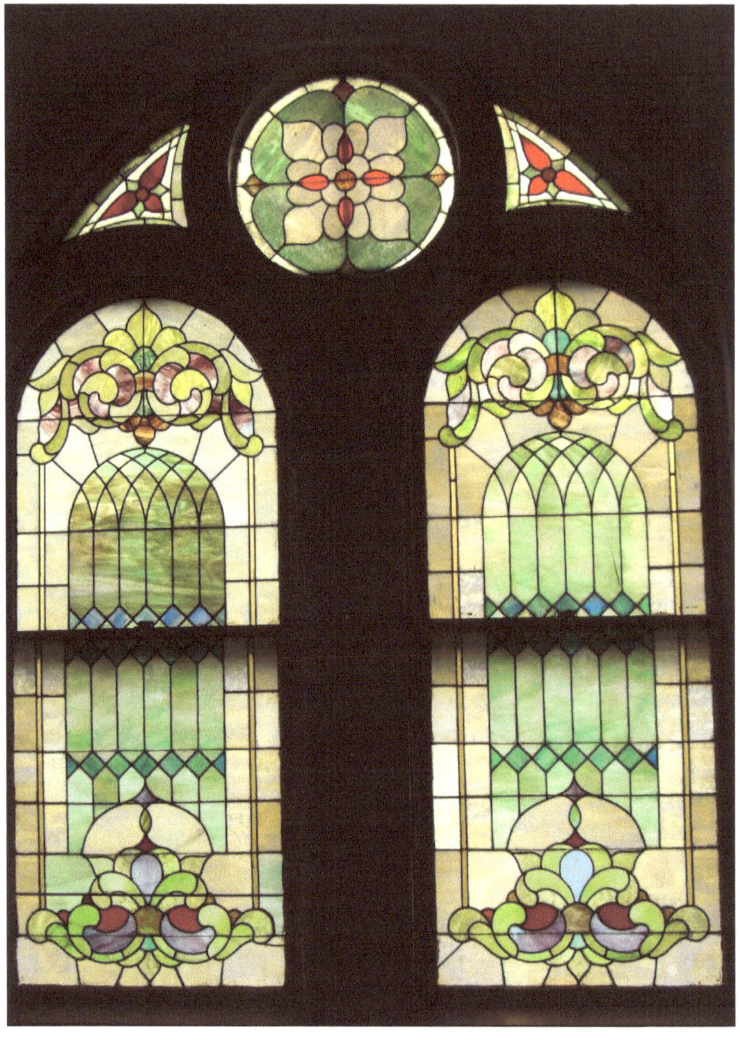

10. Second story window facing South

The second story Alder Street sanctuary window (11) contains panels of many types and varieties of stained glass, some of which have painted illustrations. A central arch representing the 'Christian Soldier' is flanked by two of opalescent glass. The three panels are topped by two round windows containing a lamp and a Bible, possibly illustrating Psalms 119:105 ("Thy word is a lamp unto my feet and a light unto my path").

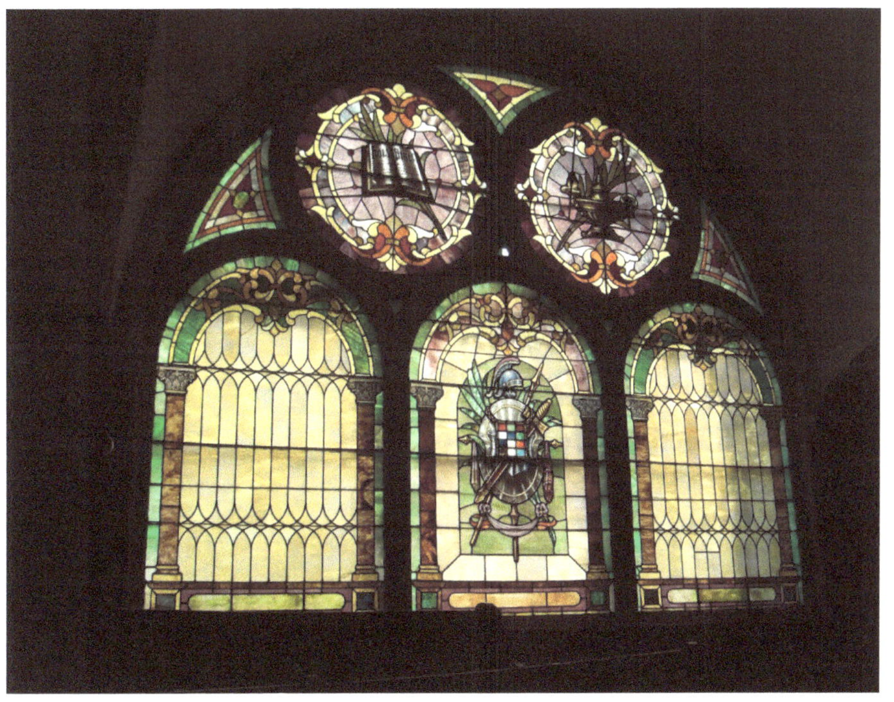

11. Second story Sanctuary window facing South

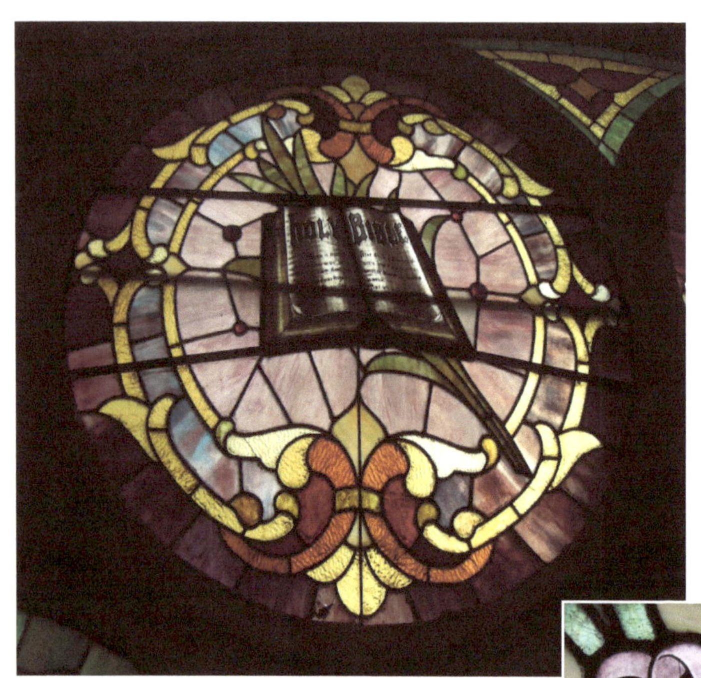

11. Details,

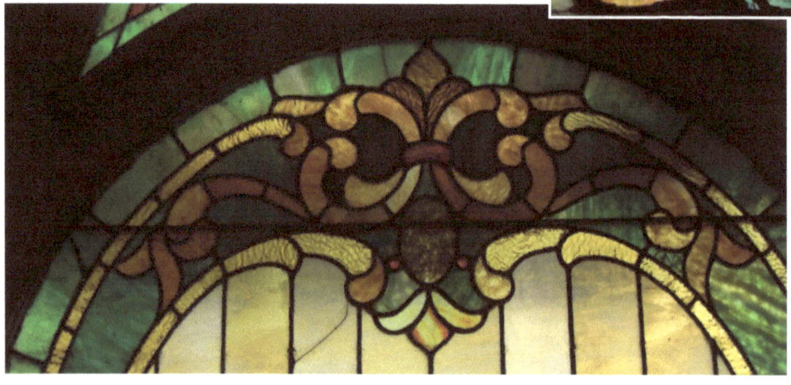

The four windows on the first floor under the large panel (12) are more elaborate than similar cross themed windows on the first and second floors of the northwest corner of the building, and transom windows at exit doors. They are frequently shaded by the big tree as seen below.

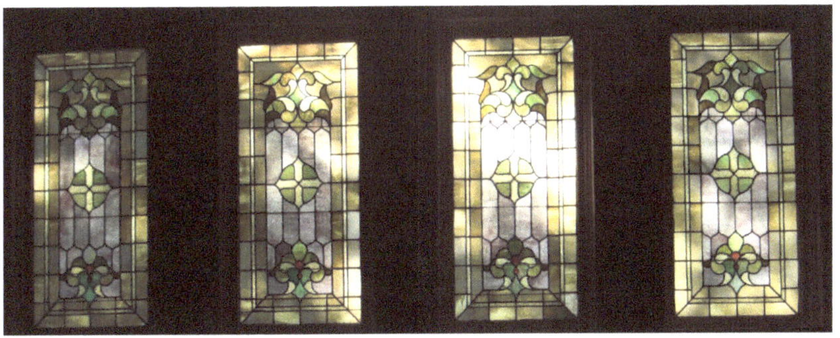

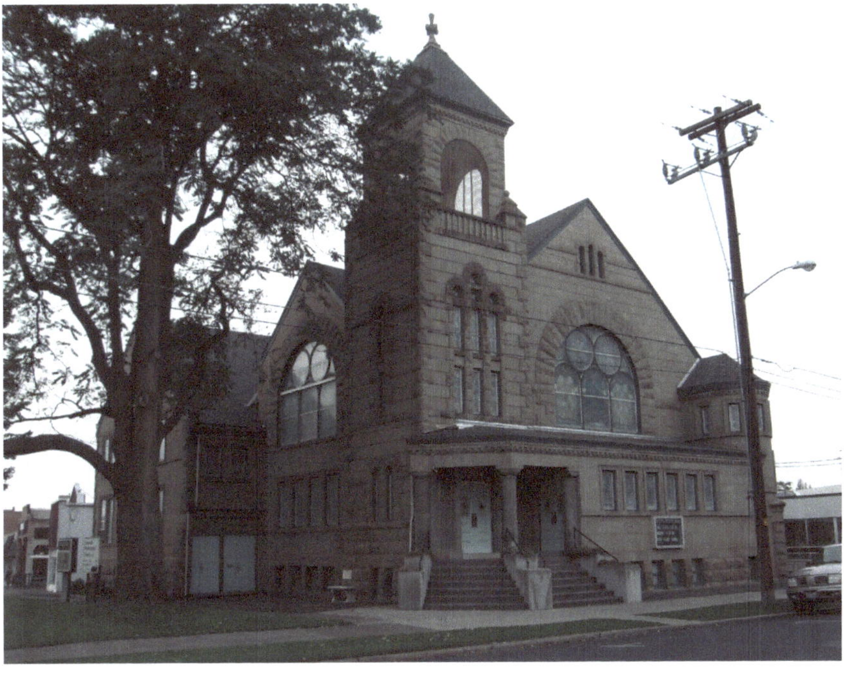

From the intersection of Alder and Palouse Streets

The main entrance to the church is at the Palouse and Alder corner of the building (13). The double doors to the south open into an enclosed vestibule that shelters the sanctuary from wind and cold, while the north side doors open into the narthex, now a cloak room that is also set up as a retreat for worshippers with small children.

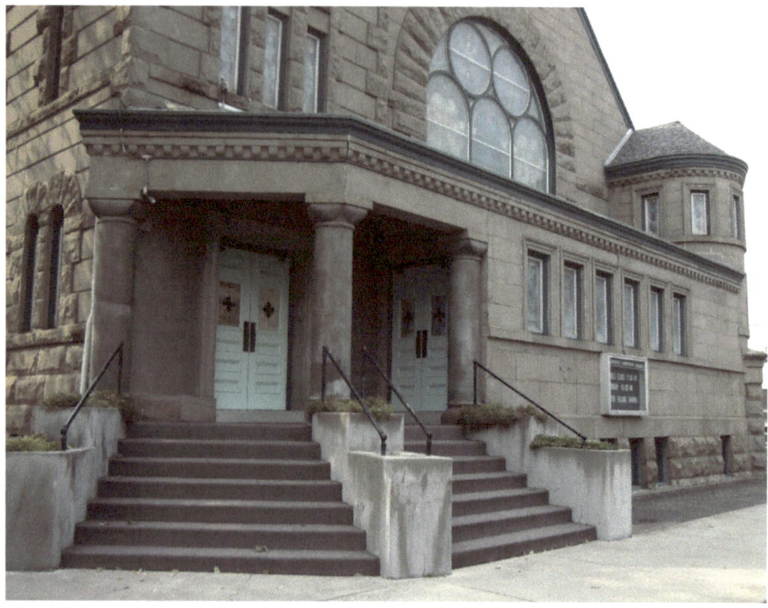

13. South-eastern external front doors. There is an inside door between the two front doors.

Doors from inside>

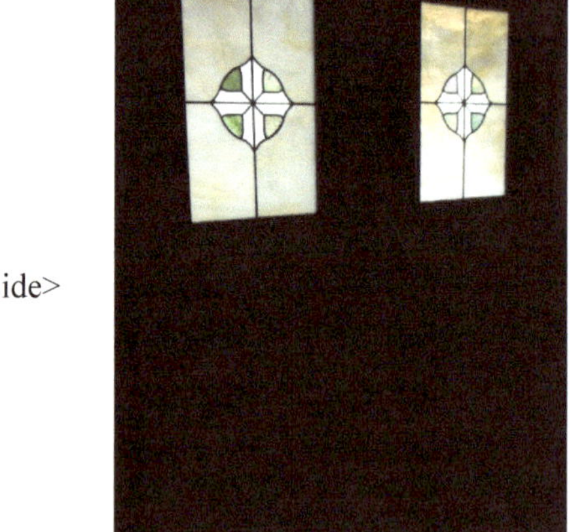

The design on the stained glass windows on the south side of the vestibule is continued up a level and repeated in the design of windows in the belfry (14). As with all the other external windows, the colors within the stained glass differ depending on the time of day and time of year, due to changes in the arc and height of the sun over the seasons.

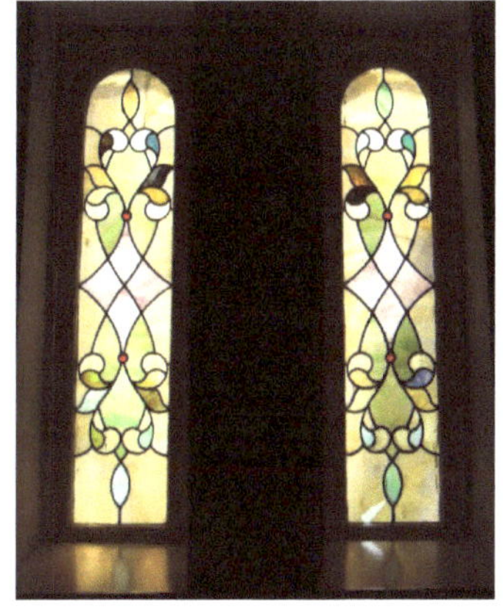

Spring

These pictures are of the same vestibule windows, taken at around 10:00 in the morning but at different times of the year 2012:

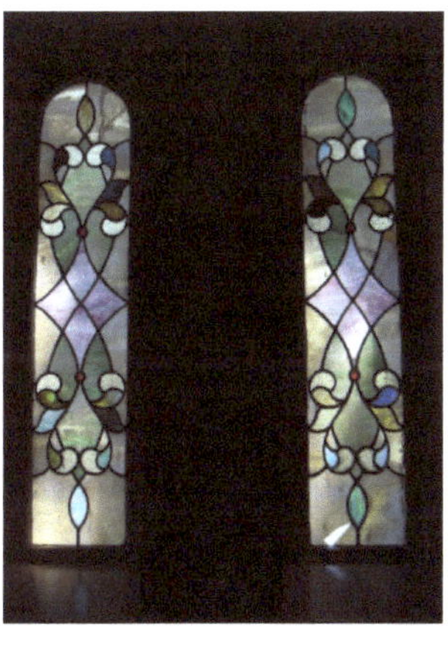

Summer

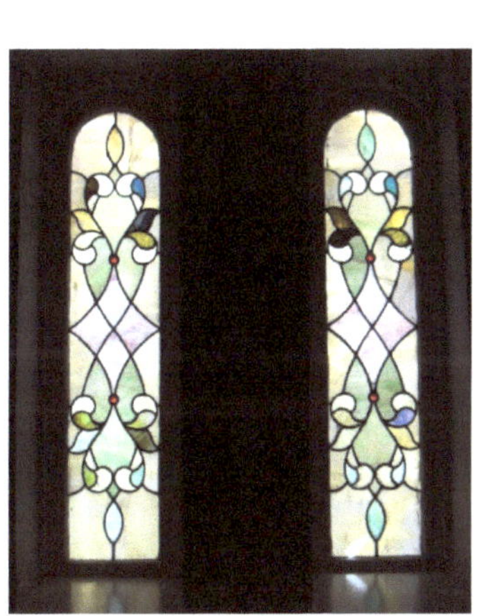

Fall

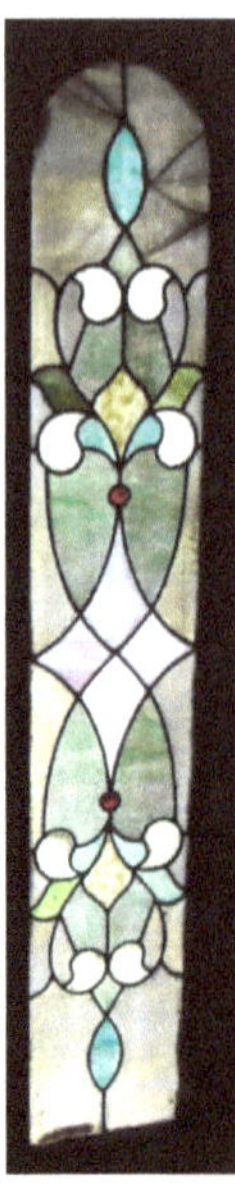

The Alder side of the belfry has two windows stacked over each other, on the second and third floors, as shown on the left.

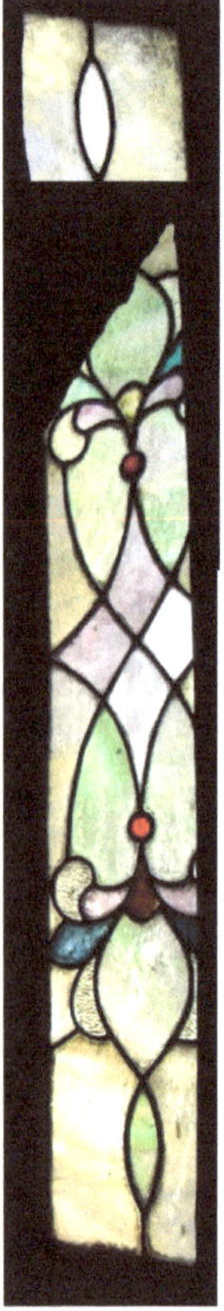

The Palouse side of the belfry has a bank of three windows at the foot of the second floor stairs into the bell tower, and a second bank of three windows topped with caps on the third floor, as seen on the right.

The belfry is currently closed.

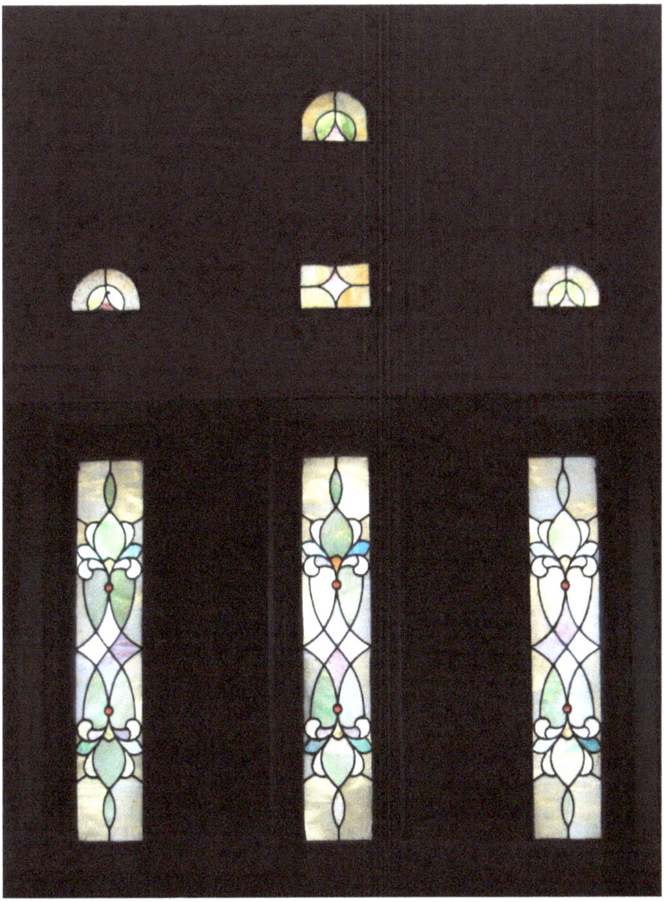

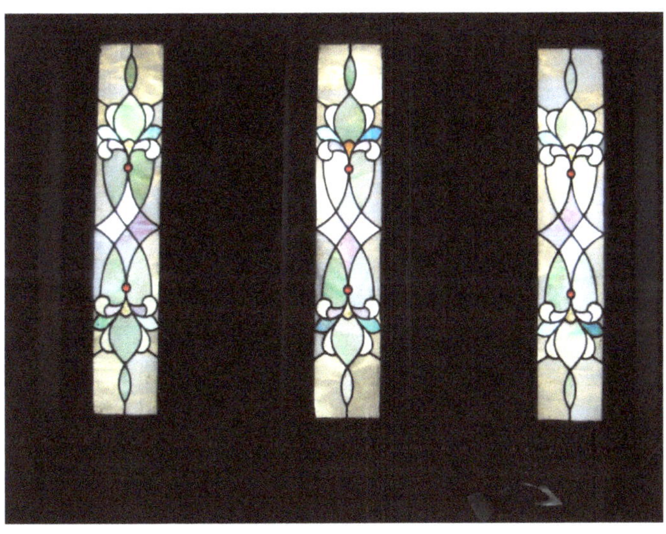

There are windows on either side of two double doors that lead from the vestibule into the sanctuary (15) which incorporate a coppery glass to outline the central crosses that looks gilded when lit by the sun. (A central window, with dove, chalice and loaf of bread, is a replacement.)

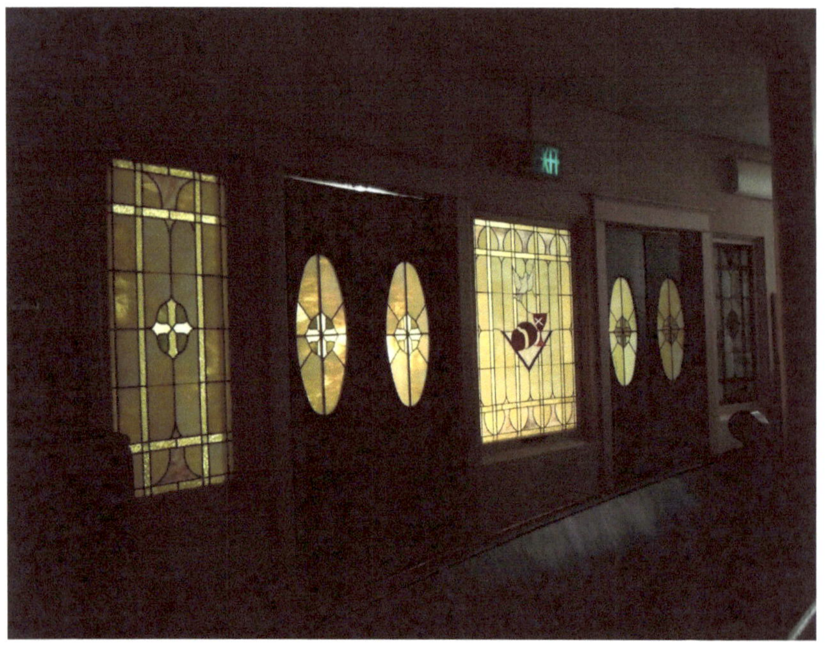

15. Entering the Sanctuary from the vestibule.

Sanctuary windows are again seen on the Palouse side of the building. In size and shape the panels (16) are equal to those on the Alder Street side. The central arch shows an empty cross against a sunset sky. The two round windows contain a palm branch with a Greek letter representing alpha and omega, possibly illustrating Revelation 1:8 ("I am Alpha and Omega, the beginning and the ending, saith the Lord, which is, and which was, and which is to come, the Almighty").

Note the tiny landscape painted on the stained glass at the base of the cross by the lily-of-the-valley. >

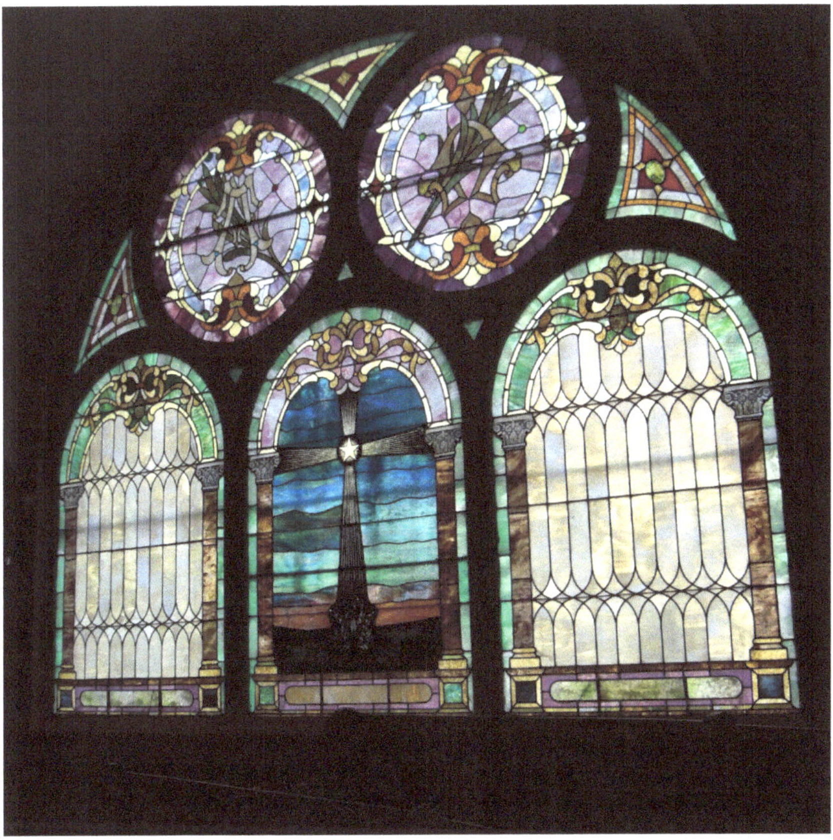

16. Second story Sanctuary window facing east. Detail below.

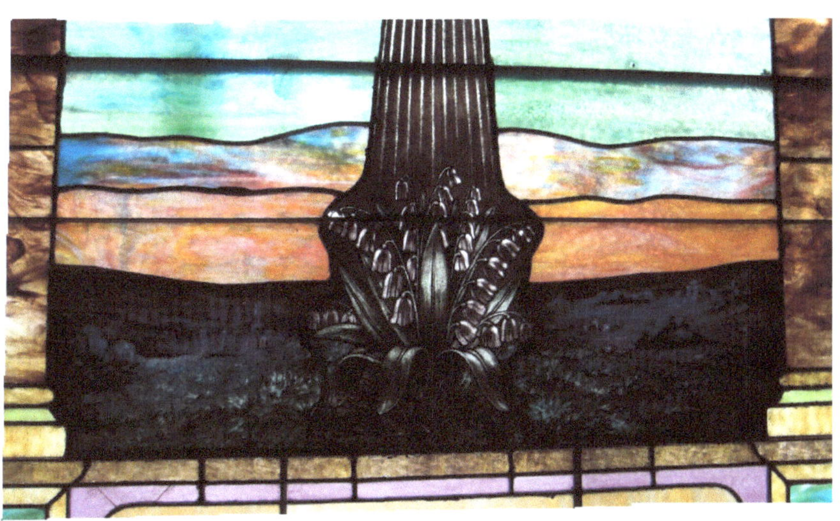

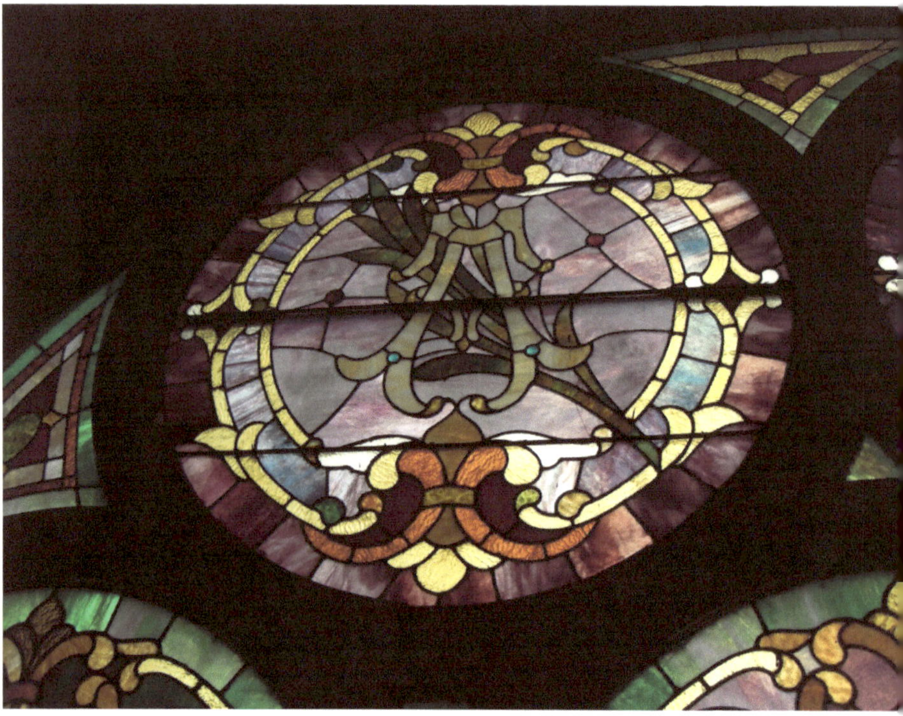

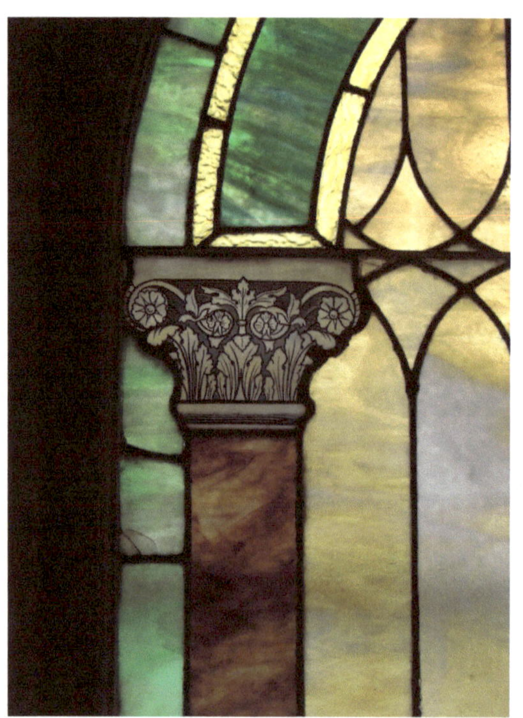

16. continued:

The interplay of cut, color, leading, the texture of different glass, light and painted detail.

The first floor bank of six windows (17) below the second floor tri-part window with the cross are in the external wall to the narthex (cloak/children's room) mentioned previously. Originally screened by three windows that were relocated, they are currently visible from the Sanctuary through three clear windows that replaced the stained glass ones.

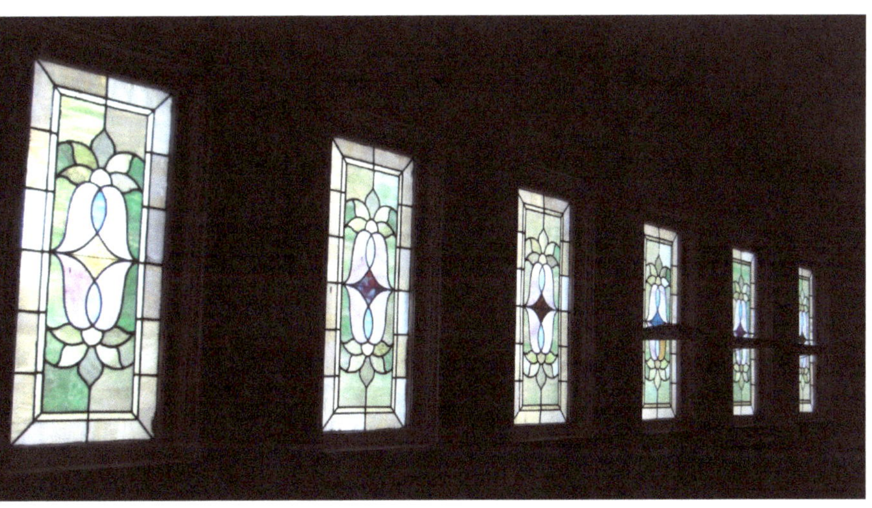

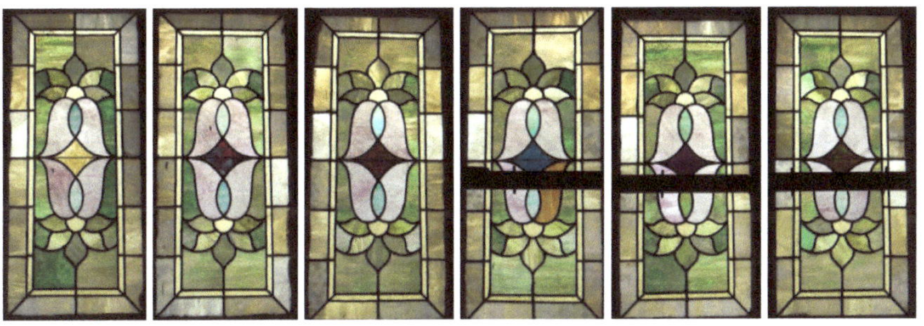

On another day, from another angle:

The turret at the Northeast side of the building houses a stairway from the basement through the second floor. A transom window (18) sits over the external ground level exit door.

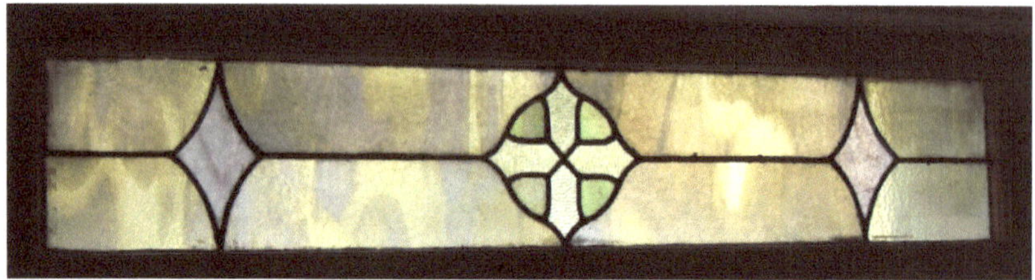

18. Above the door at the Northeast corner

There is a five panel set of windows (20) around the second floor top of the turret that accents the architectural element.

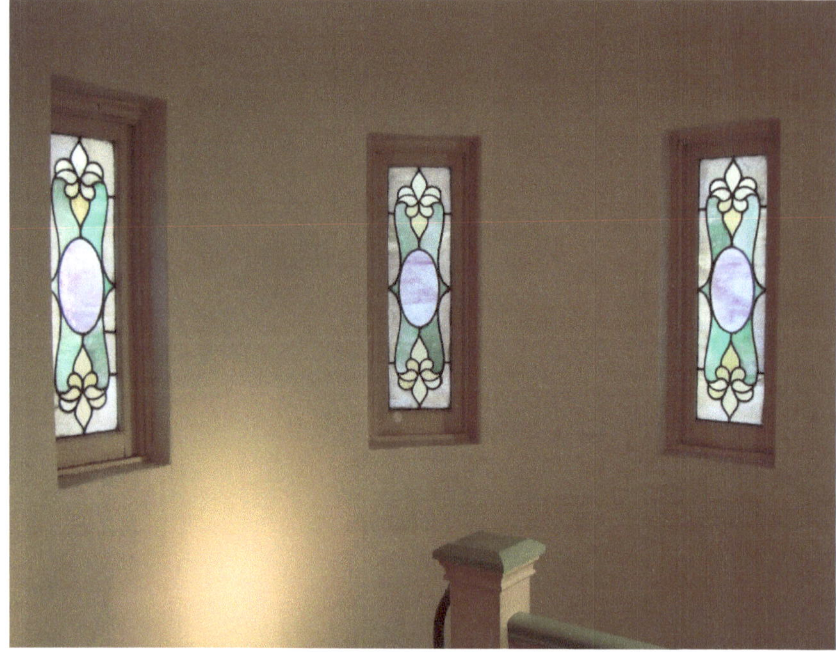

20. Three of the five panel three-quarter circle

A small window (19) provides foot light on the stairs to the second floor.

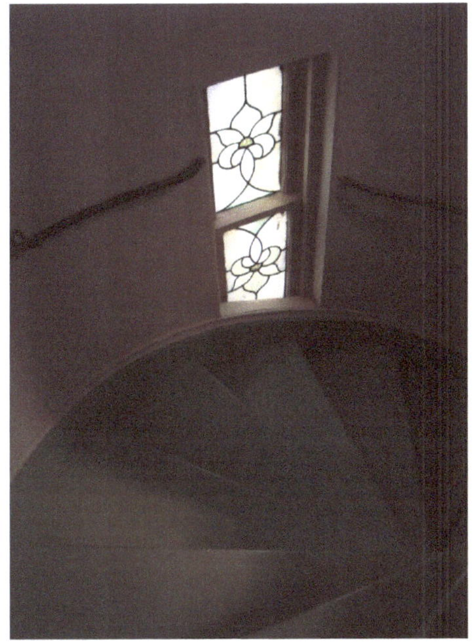

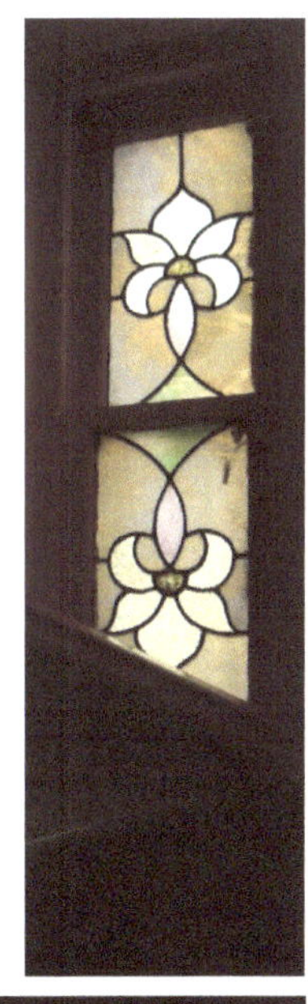

And the whole thing makes a graceful entry and exit to the Sanctuary balcony.

The turret is currently roped off and not being used.

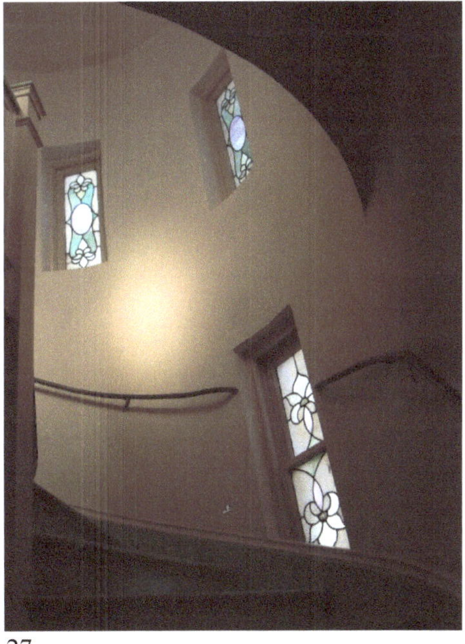

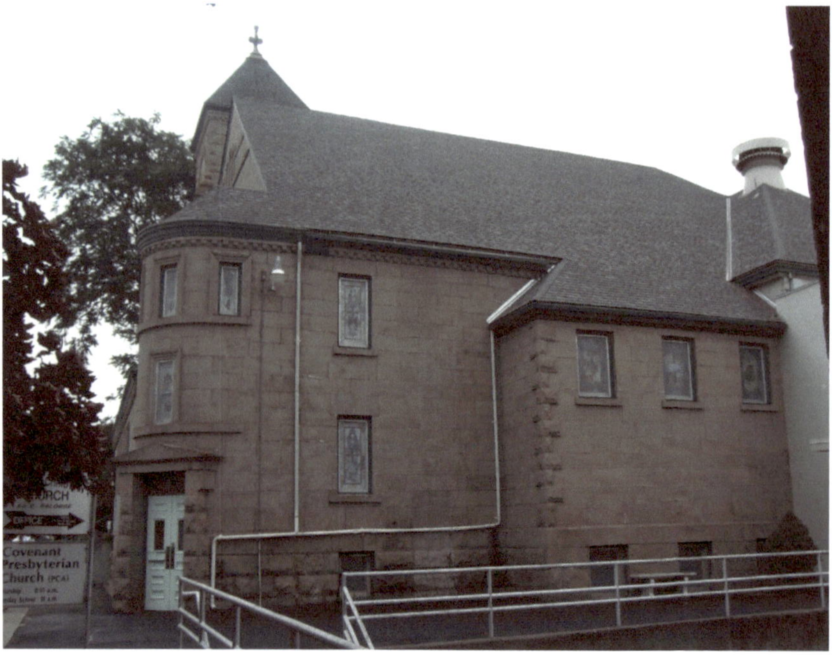

North side of the Church

There is a stained glass rectangular window on each floor of the sanctuary, on the north side just before the exit doors (21)>

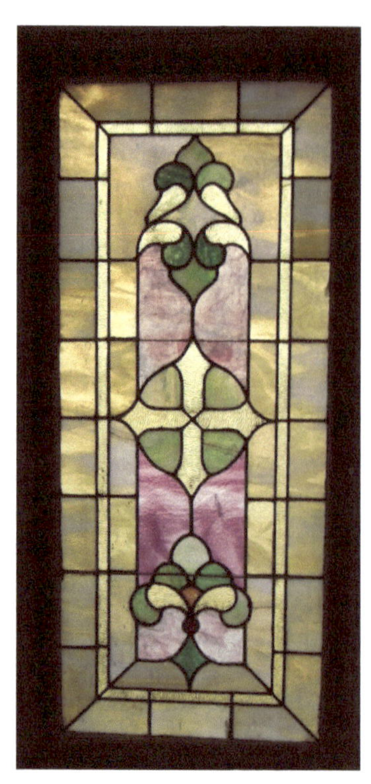

The three windows along the North side of the church (22, 23 and 24) are above the choir loft in the sanctuary. They were the result of ideas conceived by Morton Gregory, the preacher at the time of the Church's construction, although designed and built by the Povey Bros. (B)

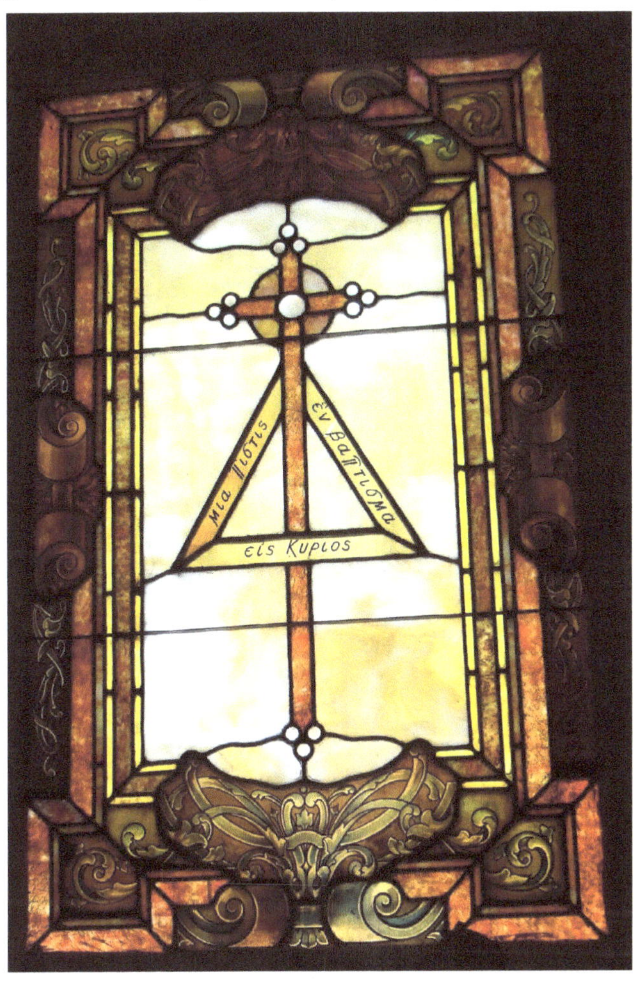

22. The 'triangle': The three phrases on the triangle are a quotation from Eph 4:5. The base line at the bottom reads "One Lord." The line on the left says "One faith," and the line on the right says, "One Baptism".

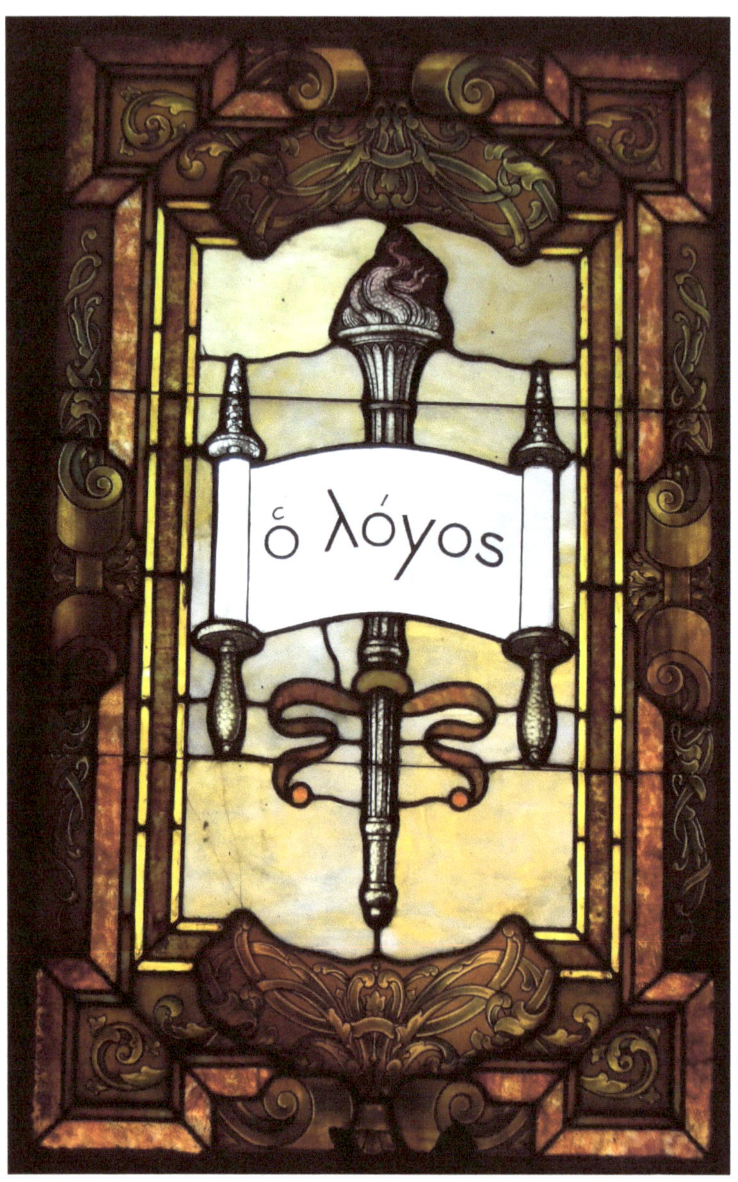

23. The 'torch and scroll': "O Logos" - Greek for "The Word" is a reference to Jesus taken from the Gospel of John chapter 1 ("In the beginning was the Word, and the Word was with God, and the Word was God"). The background is a picture of a scroll depicting the "word". This is a reference to the divinity of Jesus Christ before his incarnation as a human, as the light to mankind.

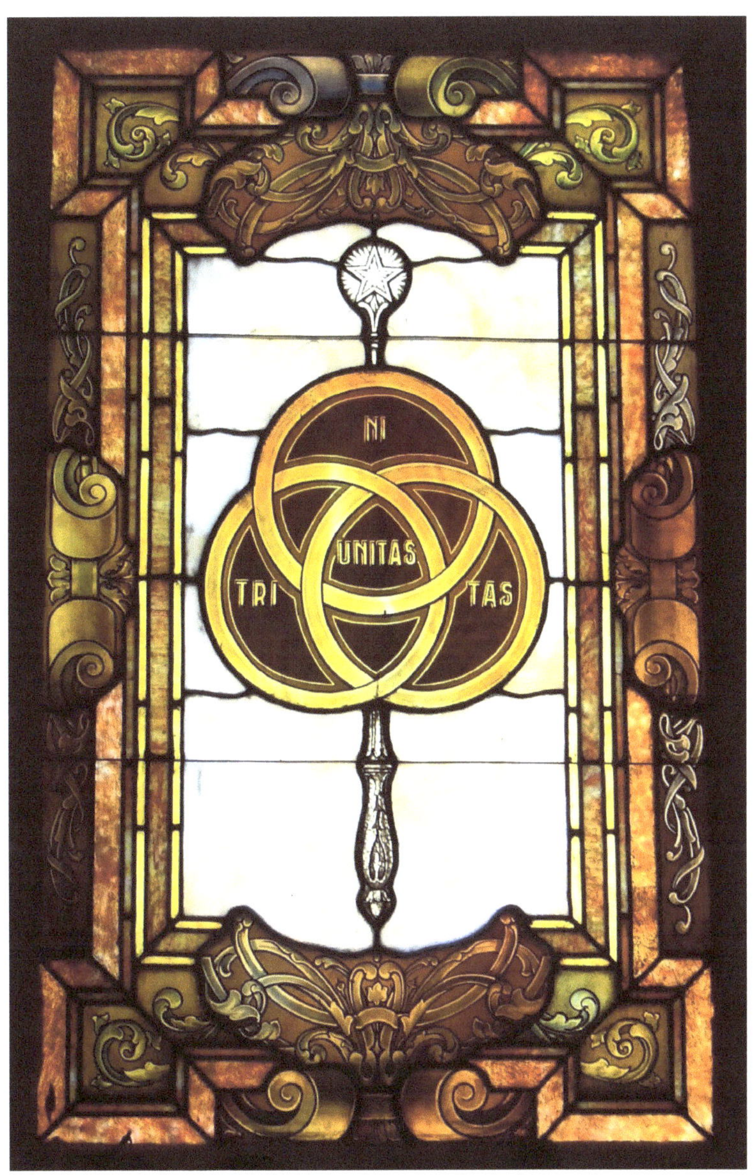

24. The 'circles':

A symbol representing the Holy Trinity: the Father, Son and Holy Ghost. In Latin. "Unitas" refers to unity or oneness, while the letters in the non-overlapping areas (Tri-ni-tas) refer to the trinity or three. Three separate entities united in one.

"The messages on all of these (Choirloft) windows are intended to lay out the basic foundation of the Christian faith." (D)

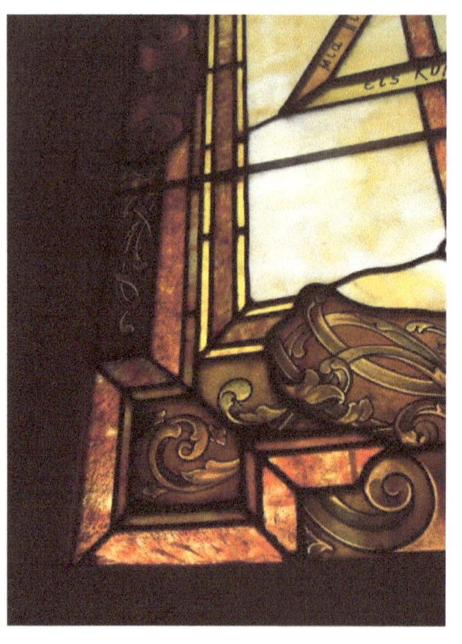

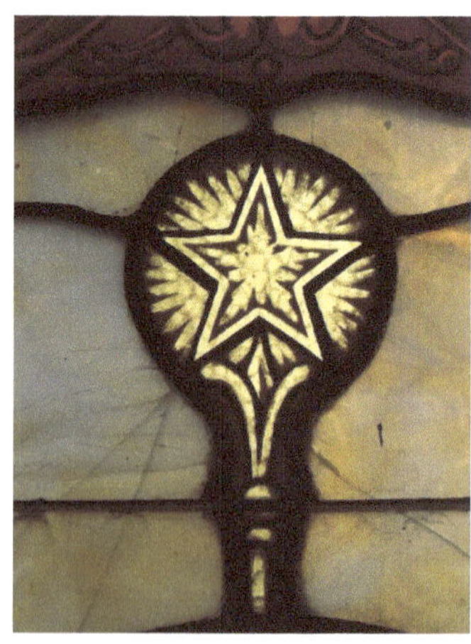

22, 23 and 24 details

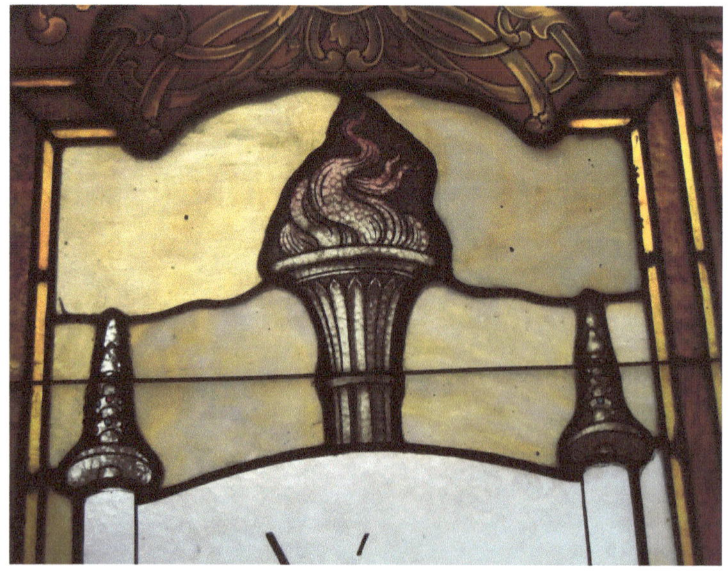

Three 'picture' windows that were relocated from the first floor (25, 26 and 27) were moved to an internal wall that divides the Sanctuary, added when the building was remodeled. They were raised to the same height as the windows in the choir-loft on the other side of the pulpit, and are lit electrically from behind.

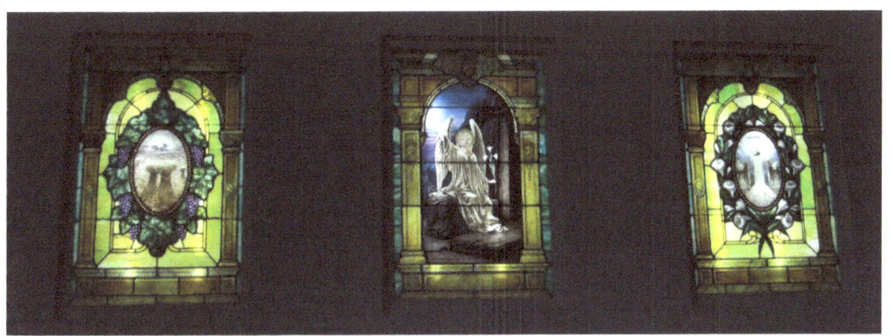

Here they are unlit

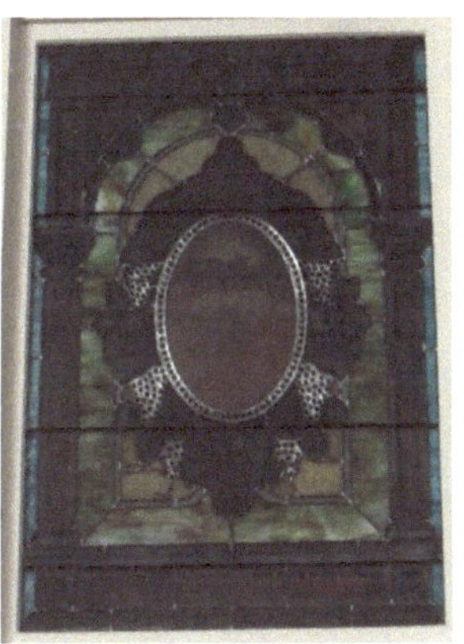

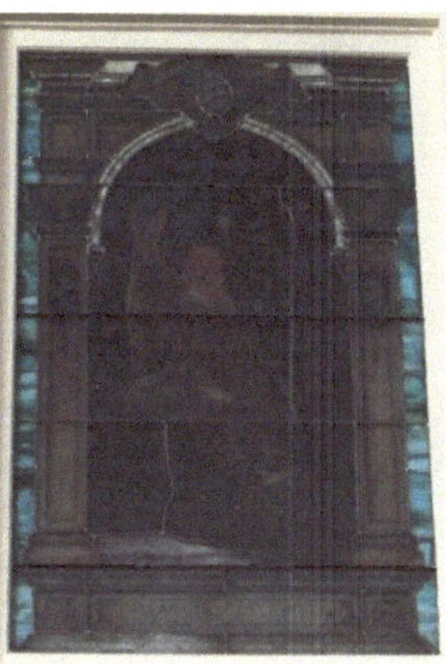

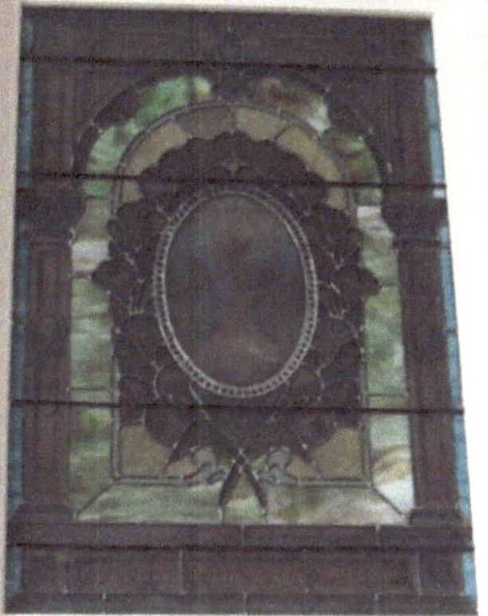

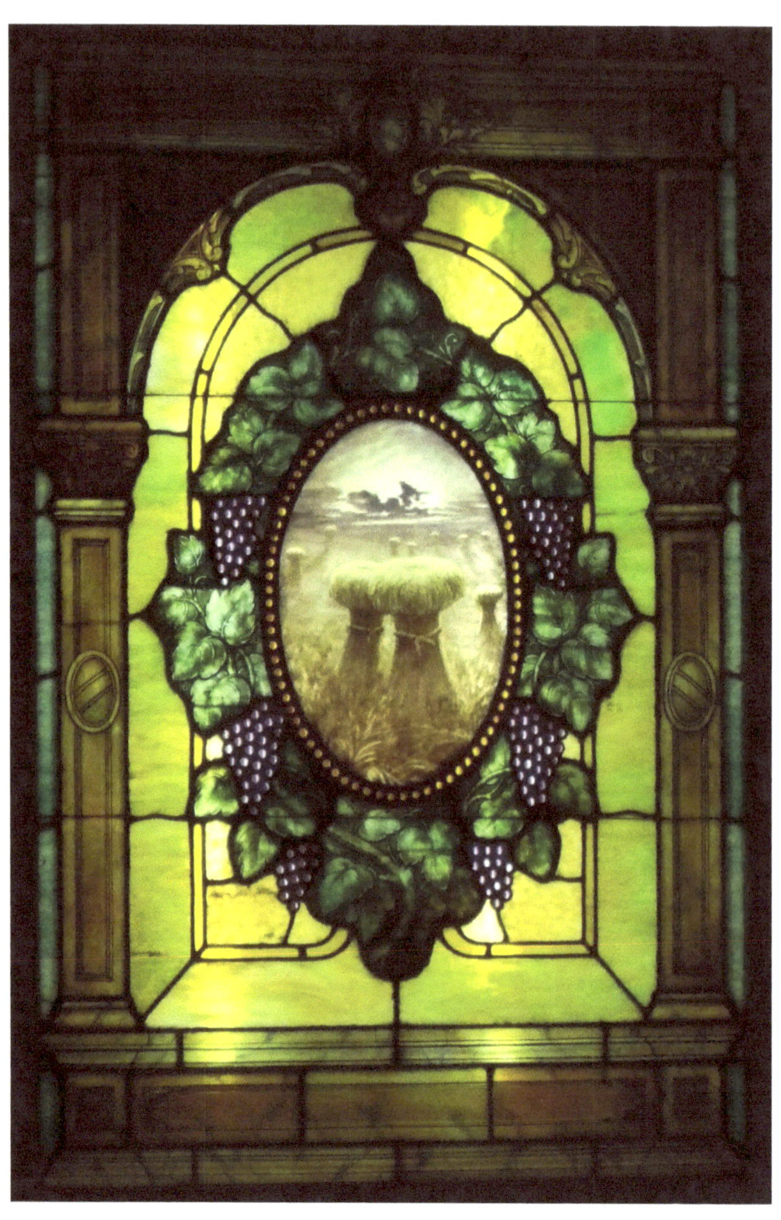

25. Wheat sheaves and grape vines represent the bread and cup of communion, and therefore the body and the blood of the new testament sacrifice as described in all four Gospels (Matthew 26:26-28 , Mark 14:22-24, Luke 22:17-19 and John 6:47-46)

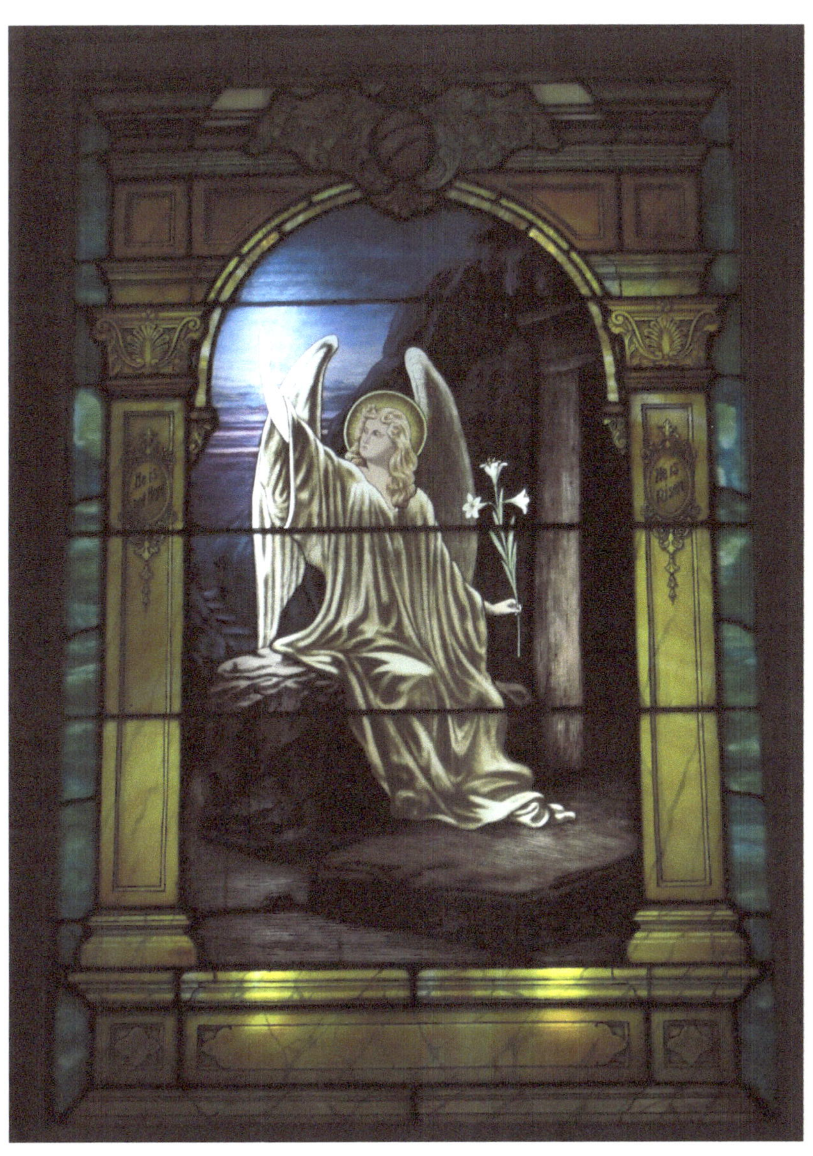

26. An Angel at the tomb when Mary Magdalene was given the Good News. Quotes on the pillars come from Matthew 28:6: "He is not here: for he has risen as he said. Come, see the place where the Lord lay".

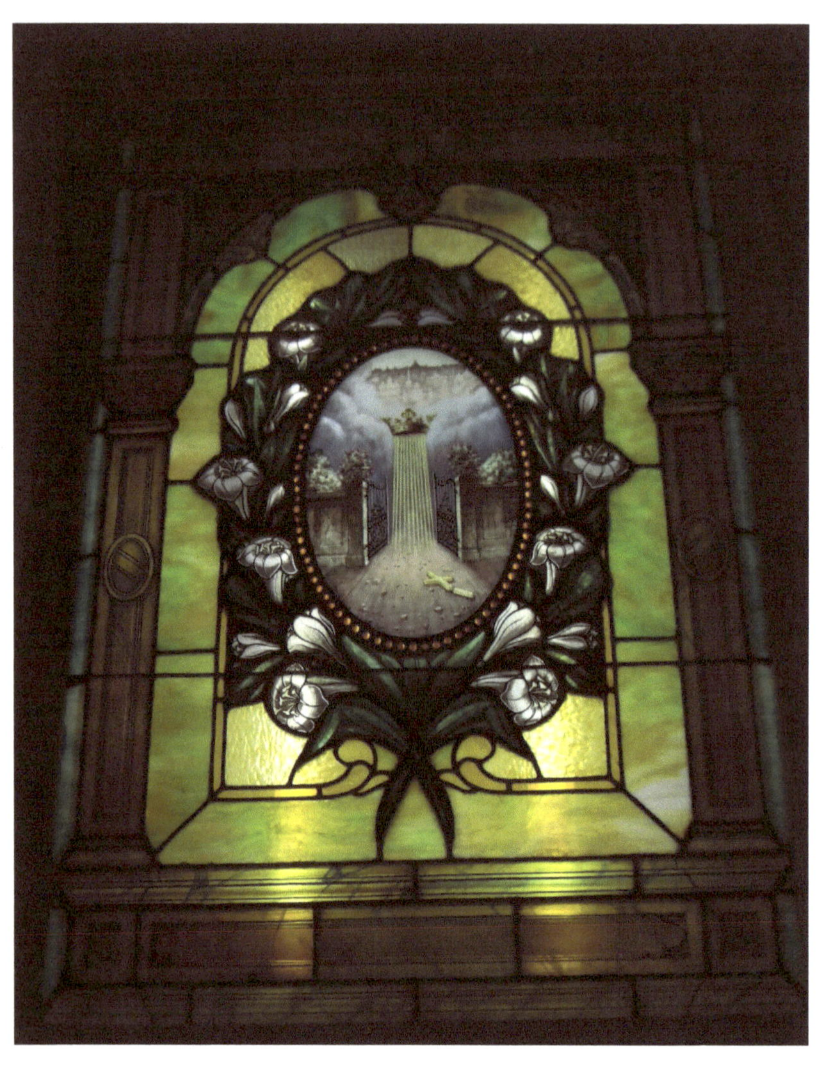

27. A broken cross and crown surrounded by lilies: illustrates resurrection, redemption and the promised triumph over death. The crown is the crown of life (as in James 1:12 and Revelation 2:19) as well as one of glory (see I Peter 5:4).

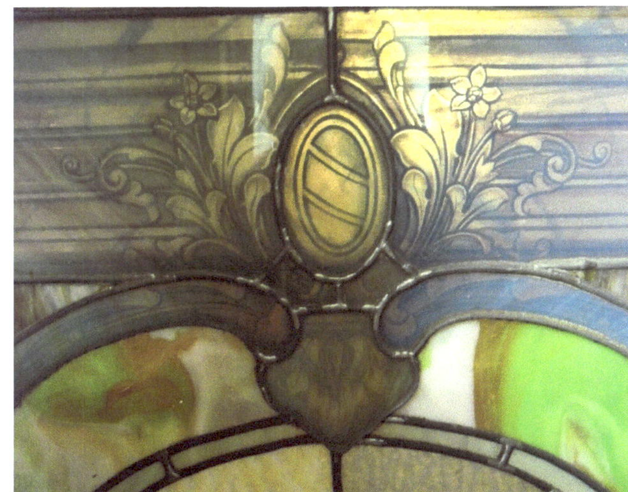

27. Details from the back of the Lilly window

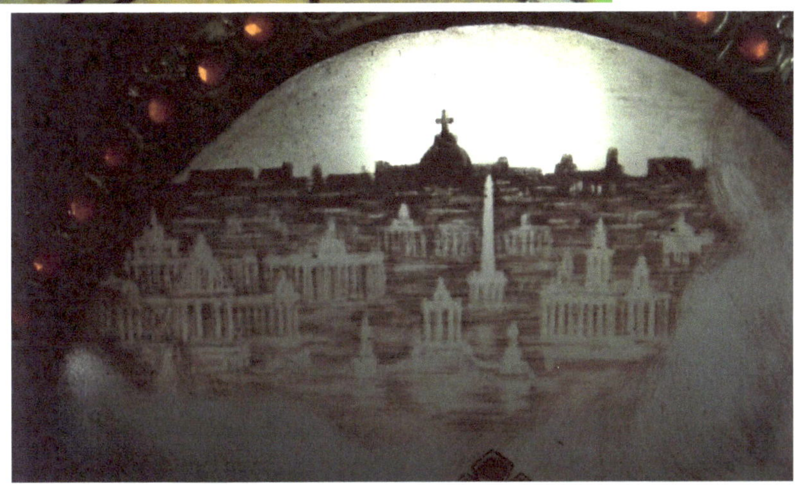

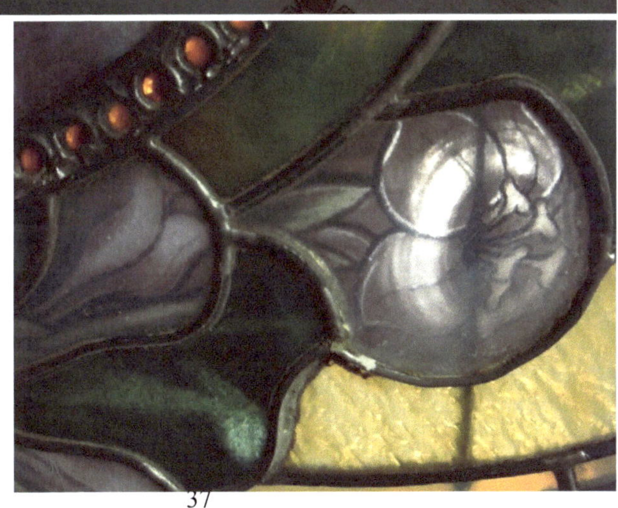

All internal swinging doors are leather covered and have the same stained glass ovals (28). There are several double doors and a few single doors inside the church.

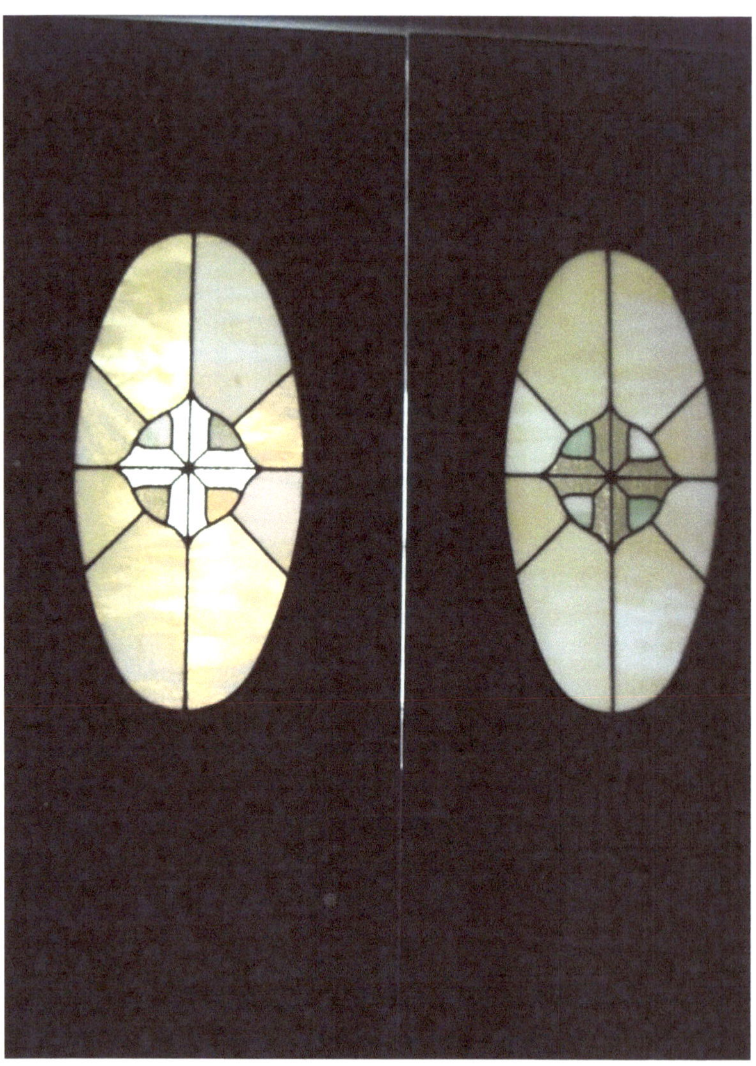

28. Internal doors from the little chapel

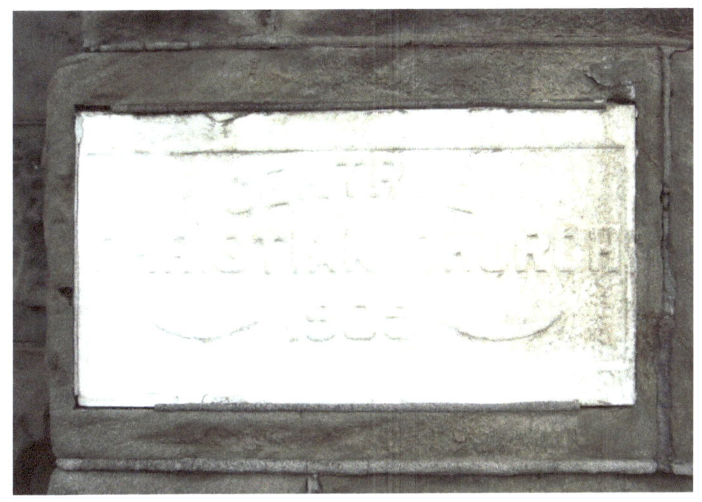

In addition to the King James version of the Holy Bible, resources consulted included:

A. Board minutes, ledgers, photographs and other archived documents which were personally examined at Central Christian Church on 7/11/12 and 10/27/12.

B. A History of Central Christian Church of Walla Walla, Washington, Compiled and edited by the Historical Committee for the 80th year celebration, 1984 .

C. McCary, Michael: "Stained Glass of the Povey Brothers Studio", public lecture 4/30/07, Architectural Heritage Center, 701 SE Grand Avenue, Portland, OR.

D. Carl P. Coseart, PhD: Professor of Biblical Studies School of Theology, Walla Walla University: personal communication.

Please note: All photographs not otherwise attributed were taken by me

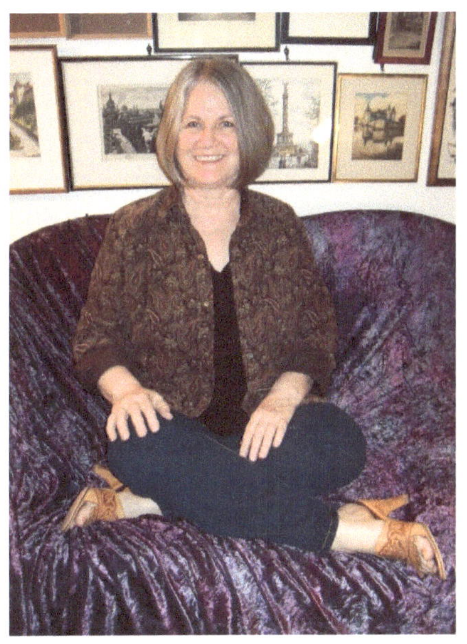

Barbara Beito now lives quietly in the State of Washington.

www.ingramcontent.com/pod-product-compliance
Lightning Source LLC
LaVergne TN
LVHW052300100826
845147LV00001B/104

* 9 7 8 0 9 8 8 6 1 5 5 1 9 *